KU KLUX KLAN:
The Invisible Empire

KU
KLUX
KLAN:
The Invisible Empire

By David Lowe

With an Introduction and Epilogue by
Haynes Johnson

W. W. Norton & Company, Inc.
New York

CONTENTS

INTRODUCTION

A S a KKK crime, it contained all the tawdry elements of the past: a defenseless victim, the mother of five children, ambushed in the darkness along a lonely road in a rural setting of swamps and Spanish moss. Violence has happened before that way in the isolated areas of the Deep South. But unlike many violent acts of that region, the murder of Viola Liuzzo in the spring of 1965 could not be ignored, for it came at the end of a series of dramatic events that had captured the attention of the world. Mrs. Liuzzo's death on the Jeff Davis Highway between Selma and the old capital of the Confederacy in Montgomery, Alabama, became both a symbol of and a catalyst for a new and intensive examination of one of America's oldest problems, the Ku Klux Klan.

The President of the United States, Lyndon Johnson, in personally announcing the arrest of four Klansmen in connection with her slaying, pledged to fight until "the hooded society of bigots" was brought under control. Congress began an investigation. Newspapers and magazines produced voluminous articles. And television turned its unique talents to the scene. This book grows out of the most memorable of those efforts to illuminate the shadowy recesses of the Klan. It is the rendering, in text and photographs, of the Emmy-Award-winning documentary, *Ku Klux Klan: The In-*

K
K
K

visible Empire, written and produced by David Lowe for CBS Reports.

On September 21, 1965, the CBS television network, with CBS News Correspondent Charles Kuralt as narrator, brought the program into millions of homes across the country.

Television, at its best, adds a new dimension to the American educational process. Although the Klan is an old and sorrowful story, never before has it been portrayed so vividly and so intimately. The cameras and microphones and the artful blending of verbatim interview and judicious commentary convey an immediacy and an understanding beyond the reach of any other medium or method. Here are the faces of fear, the words of ignorance, the venomous appeals to bigotry, the blatant commercial motivations, the chilling sight of infants being held aloft before a flaming cross to participate in their parents' world of racial and religious hatreds. It is an unforgettable portrait, and I speak from personal experience as one who has dealt with the Klan throughout the South.

I did not see the CBS production when it was originally shown and, frankly, because of my own involvement, I approached my first viewing skeptically. My reservations were swiftly swept away, however, and I became caught up again in that unbelievable yet all-too-true realm of the "Invisible Empire." This book makes available, in permanent form, some of those terrible truths that flickered across our screens. It also helps to explain why the Ku Klux Klan remains one of the most enduring problems in America, a problem that can be understood fully today only by looking first to the past.

Seldom, if ever, has an organization been founded in more ironic circumstances than the KKK. Its emblems, its paraphernalia, its name, principles, purposes, people, and, indeed, its very birthplace were the antithesis of everything the Klan was to become.

The Ku Klux Klan was born at the end of December 1865 in the small market center of Pulaski, Tennessee, a town named for that intrepid Polish fighter for American freedom, Count Casmir Pulaski. Six young men, former Confederate officers and gentlemen all, had decided to form a club, principally for their own amusement. One of them suggested the Greek word for circle, *kuklos*, which they transformed into Ku Klux; then they created a fantastic and mystical ritual to accompany their secret order. They put on masks and disguises, met surreptitiously, held exotic initiations, and roamed about the countryside at night on horseback. Before long, they discovered that their nocturnal galloping was creating fear and dread among the superstitious Negro field hands. Clearly, the Ku Klux held other than social possibilities. The idea began to spread slowly throughout

K
K
K

the South; but it wasn't until the spring of 1867 that a formal, regional KKK organization was formed.

By April 1867 the radical Republicans in Congress had divided up the South into military districts and the bitter reconstruction era of carpetbaggers and freedmen had begun. With Reconstruction came the flowering of the Ku Klux Klan. At a meeting in Nashville, Tennessee, a charter was drafted and adopted. The Klan, as it was conceived, was to be a vigilante group—but an honorable one, as befitting its membership and motives. Nathan Bedford Forrest, the grizzled and gallant Confederate general who had closed his military career at the great battle of Selma, Alabama, the last major engagement of the Civil War, was chosen as Grand Wizard. He ruled over an empire divided into realms, dominions, provinces, and dens, each headed by Grand Dragons, Titans, Giants, and Cyclops. The Klan's charter spoke of its desire to defend the weak, the innocent, the defenseless, and the oppressed, and to uphold all laws, including the Constitution of the United States. Such sentiments were in keeping with its original membership. The Klan drew into its order some of the best men of the South, many of them veterans, already proud possessors of the mystique which rapidly was growing up around those supposedly chivalrous cavaliers who had fought with Lee and ridden with Jackson.

As participants in the original "Invisible Empire," these men saw themselves as upholders of the best of their traditions, as protectors of their women, defenders of their homes. They wore white robes, the emblem of purity, and adopted the cross as their symbol. They rode across the South, driving out carpetbaggers, Yankee schoolteachers and judges, and putting Negroes in their "proper places." Inevitably, the character of the Klan changed. From warnings and threats, Klan units proceeded to violent acts—floggings, tar and featherings, mutilations, and murders. The better members dropped out; their places often were taken by those for whom violence became a cause in itself. Many of them were driven by a logical, if selfish, motivation: they were poor and ignorant whites who had the most to fear from the economic competition of free Negroes. Conditions within the Klan were deteriorating so rapidly that in January of 1869, less than two years after its regional founding, Forrest ordered the "Invisible Empire" disbanded and all of its records burned. The Klan, the general said, was becoming perverted from its original purposes, an opinion which an ardent Alabama Klansman, Ryland Randolph, strongly endorsed. To Randolph, the Klan had fallen into low and violent hands.

Disbanded officially though it was, the Klan hung on as an effective terroristic organization for another three years until, in 1872, it ceased to function in the South. It was no longer needed: Reconstruction was ending; Southerners again were ruling the South. Despite its depredations, the Ku Klux Klan received much of the

K
K
K

credit for the eventual restoration of the South. For years after, Southern boys grew up with the memories of the stirring days when their fathers, like knights of old, rode the land protecting their most valued possessions. It was a myth that went hand in hand with the other legends of the defeated Southland. Like all myths, it became ever grander and eventually, a generation later, it fired the flames of a new, more ominous revival of the KKK.

William Joseph Simmons, tall, scholarly looking in his rimless glasses, part visionary, part huckster, one-time private in the Spanish-American War who later adopted the self-imposed title of "colonel," a Methodist circuit rider and joiner of every possible fraternal organization, was sitting on a bench one day in 1901 gazing into a cloudy, windswept sky. Suddenly he saw the clouds part and form into small sections which followed one another in a mighty procession across the sky. As he would solemnly say later, it was a sign from God. Simmons fell to his knees in prayer. Visions of that ghostly procession awakened his memories of the old Klan and stirred Simmons' boyhood dreams of organizing an army of salvation. Fourteen years later his idea became reality when, on December 6, 1915, he chartered the Knights of the Ku Klux Klan in Atlanta, Georgia. The KKK, as Simmons described it, was "the world's greatest secret, social, patriotic, fraternal, beneficiary order." His timing was propitious. The Klan's rebirth came precisely at the moment of the premiere of the film *The Birth of a Nation* in Atlanta. Only days before, Simmons had shrewdly set the stage when he and sixteen followers climbed to the top of Stone Mountain, outside of Atlanta, and ignited a crudely fashioned pine cross soaked in kerosene. "Bathed in the glow of the fiery cross," he would say melodramatically, "the Invisible Empire was called from its slumber of half a century."

Simmons' match ignited the formation of the largest, most powerful vigilante organization in American history, an organization which, after numerous internal changes, survives to this day. But actually the real spark that set off the Klan in the twentieth century came first from a meteoric fellow southerner, Thomas Dixon, Jr., who had written two books shortly after the turn of the century.

Dixon had done everything: he had studied with Woodrow Wilson in the Johns Hopkins graduate school and had been, in quick succession, a lawyer, politician, actor, preacher, lecturer, and finally a writer. His books, *The Leopard's Spots* and its sequel, *The Clansman: An Historic Romance of the Ku Klux Klan,* were sensational successes. They glorified the old South and the old Klan, and threw in a saccharine love story for added interest. In Dixon's account, the North was villainous, Negroes were savages, southern gentlemen and ladies paragons,

K
K
K

the KKK ennobling. He adapted his book about the Klan to the stage, even acting in one of several touring companies, and tried to organize his own movie company to make a silent film. At that point, he fortuitously met D. W. Griffith, a young Kentuckian who was directing motion pictures for the Biograph Company. Griffith, who had been saving his own money for more ambitious productions, was enthused. He undertook the task of filming *The Clansman*. In a day of slapstick and stilted shorts, Griffith and his cameraman, Billy Bitzer, wrought a technical masterpiece that revolutionized the motion picture industry. The film, which Dixon himself had renamed *The Birth of a Nation* after seeing a preview in New York, was an unprecedented success throughout the United States. And because of its controversial subject matter and its glorification of the South and Klan, it was seen amid a glare of publicity. In some northern areas it encountered censorship difficulties; in others, prominent citizens, such as Harvard's president Charles Elliott and Jane Addams, angrily denounced it. For a time, the controversy threatened the showing of the film.

Dixon, typically, held a master key. He arranged for his old friend Woodrow Wilson, then the President, to see the film at a private showing in the White House attended by members of the Cabinet. At the end, Wilson, the southerner, said: "It is like writing history with lightning, and my only regret is that it is all so terribly true." Next, Dixon called on Supreme Court Justice Edward White. At the mention of the Klan, the old jurist said: "I was a member of the Klan, sir. . . . Through many a dark night, I walked my sentinel's beat through the ugliest streets of New Orleans with a rifle on my shoulder."

With such impeccable backing, the film—and the idea of the KKK—assumed greater stature and acceptance than it undoubtedly ever would have. It was in such a setting that "Colonel" W. J. Simmons decided to announce the rebirth of the Knights of the Ku Klux Klan. For $16.50 any pure, patriotic, native-born, white Protestant American citizen over eighteen was eligible to join the noble mystic order. Ten dollars went for the initiation fee, the remainder for a cheap white robe.

Simmons had added new touches to the old rituals. He compiled a bewildering mixture of words, titles, slogans, signals—and even a Klan calendar. Dens were governed by "Exalted Cyclops," Klaliffs," "Klokards," "Kludds," "Kligrapps," "Klagaroos," and on down to "Nighthawks"; Klansmen sang "Klodes," met at secret "klonvocations," and spoke in a mumbo jumbo of words formed from the first letters of sentences.

"Ayak," the faithful member would say. (Are you a Klansman?)

"Akia," would come the reply. (A Klansman I am.)

"Kigy," the Klansman would answer. (Klansman, I greet you.)

K
K
K

These salutations and titles continue in Klan use today.

By 1920 Simmons' Klan had spread throughout Georgia and into Alabama, but its membership was still small, probably no more than six thousand. Simmons, in the modern parlance, was an idea man, but not an effective organizer. That spring he found his organizers in the unlikely persons of Edward Young Clarke and Mrs. Elizabeth (Bessie) Tyler, two publicists and professional fund raisers in Atlanta. Together they operated what they called the Southern Publicity Association. Clarke, an intense, nervous, former newsman, then was promoting a harvest home festival in Atlanta, and Mrs. Tyler, heavy-set, who had been married for the first time at the age of fourteen, was publicizing a "better babies" parade. Neither was an attractive person; neither had been successful up to that point. But they had the necessary talents for the Ku Klux Klan.

Simmons turned over the organizational and fund-raising activities to them. For their efforts, they would receive eight dollars of every ten-dollar initiation fee. They divided the country into eight "domains," each headed by a Grand Goblin, and subdivided the domains into "realms," or states, each headed by a Grand Dragon. Then they began their promotional efforts. What happened next remains one of the most remarkable, and disturbing, chapters in American history.

Within a year and a half, the KKK had gained more than one hundred thousand members—and was expanding rapidly across the country, into the northeast as far as Maine, on the Pacific coast north to Oregon. Enlistments were pouring in at the rate of five thousand a day. Money filled the coffers. At that point nothing could stop the Klan.

A heralded Klan exposé by the crusading *New York World* in September 1921 only spurred recruitment. The newspaper's articles were reprinted in some twenty papers; often, new Klan members would write to Atlanta headquarters saying they had heard of the KKK through the paper and wanted to join. A congressional investigation in October 1921 by the House Rules Committee, stimulated by the *World's* articles, gave the order still more publicity. Eventually, Simmons would say: "Congress gave us the best publicity we ever got. Congress made us."

In fact, no single factor "made" the Klan. The Klan's phenomenal success in the twenties grew out of the climate of the times: the emotional letdown from the fervor of World War I; fear of the Bolsheviks and the hysteria that followed the Wall Street bombing and the raids of Wilson's Attorney General, A. Mitchell Palmer; the race riots in the North and South; the migration of millions of Negroes from the old Southland into the urban centers of the North, and the talk of a "new

K
K
K

Negro"; concern over the rising Catholic population and the possibility that a Catholic, Al Smith of New York, might be President; distrust of foreigners and aliens as subversive and "un-American"; and a vague discontent, an ill-defined unhappiness with the rapidly changing America. The Klan fed on ignorance, fear, jingoism, nativism, conformism. As Sinclair Lewis had already pointed out in *Main Street,* these were all powerful factors in American life. Perhaps Frederick Lewis Allen said it best. The Klan, he wrote, provided "a chance to dress up the village bigot and let him be a Knight of the Invisible Empire. The formula was perfect."

Far more alarming, though, was the scope of the power the Klan was able to wield. At its peak, in 1924, some four and a half million Americans were members of the KKK and the "Invisible Empire" was a dominant political force in Oregon, Oklahoma, Texas, Arkansas, Indiana, Ohio, and California, to say nothing of the traditional Deep South states. The Klan helped to elect governors and senators, mayors and councilmen, and its influence was felt in Washington.

Indeed, the Klan had assumed such power that many joined as an expedient, or political, measure. Among them in that year of 1922 was the former World War I artillery captain and haberdasher, Harry S. Truman, later the President. In that same period, a young lawyer in Birmingham, Alabama, Hugo Black, now a

K
K
K

Supreme Court Justice, became a member of the KKK.*

The Klan reached its apogee in 1924, when its membership and power were decisive factors in the Democratic national convention. In perhaps the most divisive political convention in United States presidential politics, the issue of the Klan shattered the Democratic Party and led to a bitter deadlock between Al Smith and William Gibbs McAdoo, Wilson's son-in-law, which was resolved eventually by selecting a compromise candidate, John W. Davis. Before the presidential balloting had begun, the convention had been torn apart on a resolution to condemn political secret societies and, specifically, the Ku Klux Klan. The debate was long and stormy, and when the ballots were tabulated the amendment to name the Klan had lost by only a single vote—542 3/20 to 541 3/20.

Within a year the Klan's membership was beginning to slip. As a way to keep up its flagging momentum and demonstrate its still sizable power, a KKK march was staged in the nation's capital. From midday until

---

*Truman had joined during a judgeship campaign, but quickly withdrew and did not receive Klan support when he ran —and lost—the next time. Black, whose Klan membership became a *cause celèbre*, had been a member for two years, and later in the twenties once publicly thanked Klansmen for making his election to the U.S. Senate possible. He became, of course, a distinguished justice and civil libertarian.

K
K
K

dusk on a hot Saturday in August more than forty thousand Klansmen, men and women, robed, carrying flags, marching sixteen to twenty abreast, paraded along the inaugural route of the Presidents to the strains of "Onward Christian Soldiers." They had come in chartered trains and buses, and by car, from all over the country. An indication of the national character of the Klan was seen in the geographical distribution of the Klansmen. The largest number came not from the South, but the North. A year later, in 1926, a second march on Washington was held; that time only half as many Klansmen journeyed to the capital. In two more years, the Catholic Smith had received his party's presidential nomination and, as the Depression era began, the Klan had ceased to function as a significant political force in the United States.

Its rise and fall had been sudden, dramatic, and dangerous.

In the end, the Klan began to dissolve from its own inequities—and from the public's knowledge of a number of scandals that discredited top leaders. E. Y. Clarke and Bessie Tyler, it was brought out, had once been arrested "at midnight in their sleeping garments, in a notorious underworld resort," and charged with disorderly conduct and possession of liquor. Clarke later was arrested for violation of the Mann and Volstead Acts. Simmons was overthrown in a highly publicized coup led by a rotund dentist from Dallas, Hiram W. Evans. But, the public learned, Simmons' pain over his dethronement had been assuaged by the payment of a $146,500 lump sum—a figure attesting to the commercial manipulations which lay behind the Klan. David W. Stephenson, the Grand Dragon of Indiana and one of the most powerful Klan leaders, who once had boasted before some twenty thousand cheering Klan supporters in Kokomo that he had been delayed because "the President of the United States kept me unduly long counseling upon vital matters of state," was arrested and imprisoned after a sordid episode involving a young woman. Stephenson had forced her into a train and brutally assaulted her. The girl took bichloride-of-mercury tablets and died. In scores of other areas Klan frauds were thoroughly exposed. A number of newspapers and individual reporters, many of them in the Deep South, collectively wrote one of the brightest, most courageous pages in journalistic history during the twenties in personally exposing the Klan.*

Finally the public came to realize that the supposed Christian order was merely a mask for vicious hoodlums and merchants of hate. During the 1930's and

---

*The New York World, Memphis Commercial-Appeal, Columbus (Ga.) Enquirer-Sun, Montgomery (Ala.) Advertiser, and Indianapolis Times won Pulitzer Prizes for their exposures of the Klan in those years and others, among them the Macon (Ga.) Telegraph and William Allen White's Emporia (Kans.) Gazette, equally deserved the honor.

throughout World War II the KKK degenerated into a small, if still dangerous, group of hardened racists in the rural Deep South.

Still, as subsequent events soon demonstrated, the Klan never entirely died. Like a snake whose head has been cut off, its body still writhed. Within a decade after World War II, the Klan once more had become a virulent force in American life.

In many respects, the resurgence of the Klan in the mid-twentieth century was inevitable. The racial revolution in the South, as exemplified first by the Supreme Court's 1954 decision striking down public school segregation and subsequently by the beginning of the Negro's own militant civil rights movement in 1956, posed a threat to the very heart of the Southern system of separation of the races. Even the moderates were disturbed at the sudden changes, and by what they interpreted to be the menacing moves of the federal authorities in Washington. The Klan fed on these fears.

From its hard-core, unregenerate, ever-present racist elements, the KKK was able to attract others who were led to believe they were fighting the last battle for the mythical "Southern way of life." The result was a climate of hatred spreading rapidly across the South— primarily in the rural South, where most Negroes lived. The Klan, in this rebirth, was confined almost exclusively to the Deep South.

Out of the new Klan movement has come a decade of disturbance and violence.

Statistics tell only part of the story. In the ten-year period from 1955 to 1965 some one thousand instances of racial violence, reprisal, and intimidation were reported. In the same period, 225 bombings occurred, many of them of churches, and more than 40 persons connected with the civil rights movement in the South were murdered. The glossary of trouble spots has grown steadily: Birmingham, Alabama, and Jacksonville, Florida; Oxford, McComb, and Philadelphia, Mississippi; Bogalusa, Louisiana, and Albany, Georgia. Once again, fiery crosses lighted the skies of countless Southern communities (a thousand flamed in one month alone in 1960) and hooded nightriders rode again, leaving terror and destruction in their wake. Floggings and brandings, castrations and other barbaric acts were employed as the Klan's weapon of coercion. Law enforcement agencies, and the bench, were successfully infiltrated by the Klan, often making it impossible to bring known offenders to justice. In some communities the breakdown in law and order was total: the Klan provided the only effective force.

I remember sitting one day in a crowded room in Jackson, Mississippi, listening as witness after witness told members of the U.S. Civil Rights Commission of vicious beatings and whippings throughout that state. One phrase was repeated again and again as a mournful

K
K
K

refrain: "No arrests have been made." Finally, after hearing obviously more than he could stomach, the gentle Father Theodore M. Hesburgh, president of Notre Dame University, said quietly: "It's one of the most savage situations I've heard of in my life."

That savagery continued unabated into 1965. As the civil rights revolution grew in size and strength, and as the new civil rights acts were placed on the national statute books, the Klan was reponding with increasing violence. Often the principal target became white Southerners themselves, those ministers, lawyers, editors, teachers, and businessmen who were attempting to lead their region out of the past. After a series of dramatic encounters between civil rights advocates and the inheritors of the Confederate legend, all the disparate forces came together in what became a historic upheaval.

Ironically, the battle was held in Selma, Alabama, the scene of Nathan Bedford Forrest's—and the Confederacy's—last stand. One hundred years later Selma, then a slumbering trading center beside the Alabama River in the heart of the rural "black belt" of the Deep South, became the scene of an emotional confrontation between black and white, old and new. It was in the aftermath of Selma that Viola Liuzzo, who had been transporting civil rights workers in her car from Selma to Montgomery, was murdered. Once more, the nation was introduced to the menace of the Ku Klux Klan and to some of the men, the scenes, and the conversations that are reproduced in the following pages that examine the present *Ku Klux Klan: The Invisible Empire.*

HAYNES JOHNSON

March 10, 1967, Washington, D. C.

KU KLUX KLAN:
The Invisible Empire

CAST OF CHARACTERS

Richmond Flowers, Attorney General of Alabama at the time of this examination of the Klan.

J. Robert Jones, Grand Dragon of the North Carolina realm of the United Klans.

The late Matt Murphy, Grand Klonsel.

A Night-hawk.

Mr. Outlaw, Grand Klexter to J. Robert Jones.

The late W. O. Eaton. Eaton, with Eugene Thomas and Collie Leroy Wilkins, was arrested and charged with the murder of Mrs. Viola Liuzzo.

Eugene Thomas.

Collie Leroy Wilkins.

Reverend Roy Woodle, Klan Kludd
who defected from the United Klans.

Robert Shelton, Imperial Wizard,
United Klans, Knights of the KKK.

Calvin Craig, Grand
Dragon of the Georgia
realm of the United Klans.

Robert Scoggins, Grand Dragon of the South Carolina realm of the United Klans.

E. L. McDaniel, Grand Dragon of the Mississippi realm of the United Klans.

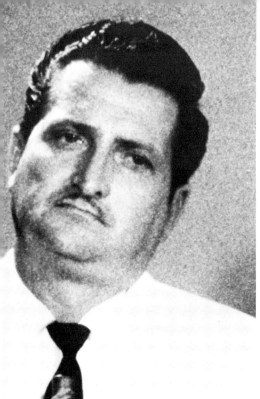

Don Cothran, Grand Dragon of the Florida realm of the United Klans.

Raymond Anderson, Grand Dragon of the Tennessee realm of the United Klans.

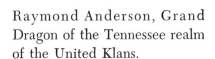

K
K
K

James Venable, Imperial Wizard, National Knights of the KKK.

Judge Daniel Duke of Georgia, fighter against the Ku Klux Klan.

Reverend Connie Lynch. ". . . the niggers in St. Augustine got quiet and went back to nigger-town where they belong."

Ralph McGill, publisher of the *Atlanta Constitution*.

Sheriff Lawrence Rainey, Neshoba County, Mississippi. He was among those indicted for the murder of three civil rights workers near Philadelphia, Mississippi.

Nicholas deB. Katzenbach, then United States Attorney General.

Representative Edwin Willis, chairman of the HUAC subcommittee investigating the Klan.

Representative Charles L. Weltner, who withdrew from the political scene rather than support Lester Maddox, segregationist governor of Georgia.

Charles Kuralt, CBS News Correspondent.

TCBS NEWS CORRESPONDENT
CHARLES KURALT:

he driver of this car was Mrs. Viola Liuzzo, mother of five children. Twenty miles from Selma, Alabama, on Route 80, a red and white sedan overtook her car. Several shots were fired. The driverless car veered off the highway and came to a stop at a cattle fence. Mrs. Liuzzo was dead. Arrested and charged with murder were three alleged members of the Ku Klux Klan. One was tried and the jury was unable to reach a verdict.

The earthen dam at left was the temporary grave of three civil rights workers, two white, one Negro—Mickey Schwerner, Andrew Goodman, and James Chaney—beaten and shot to death. Among those indicted for this triple slaying were six men identified as members of the Ku Klux Klan. None has been brought to trial.

In the automobile above, Reserve Lieutenant Colonel Lemuel Penn was killed by a shotgun blast while riding through Colbert, Georgia. Arrested for this crime were four Knights of the Ku Klux Klan. Two Klansmen were tried and acquitted.

In a few short months: five murders, thirteen alleged members of the Ku Klux Klan said to be involved in the killings.

K
K
K

Attorney General Richmond Flowers
of Alabama:

When such an order as this moves in and takes over
the police power, you are completely at their mercy, and
their atrocities and their violence can be visited on anybody that disagrees with them in any given situation.

Kuralt:

What started as a joke a hundred years ago when a
group of men donned bedsheets for a romp has over the
years attracted to it persons charged with acts of har-
rassment, intimidation, and violence throughout the

South. Even though the nation has been outraged for many years, the Ku Klux Klan persists with its bizarre ritual and trappings. But a hundred years is a long time for a joke.

Virtually every President of the United States in the past century has said the Klan has little regard for constituted authority. President Johnson, following the murder of Mrs. Liuzzo in Alabama, defined the Ku Klux Klan as a "hooded society of bigots" and warned Klansmen to get out of the Klan and return to a decent society before it is too late.

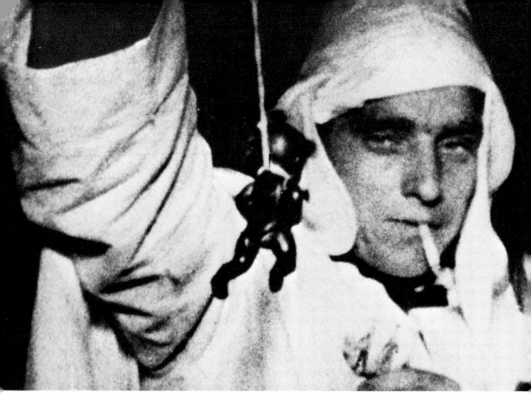

After the President's warning, the House Un-American Activities Committee started a full-scale investigation of the Klan and open hearings are scheduled for next month.* The hearings will present witnesses—not only Klansmen but also victims of Klan activity. However, the committee will not attempt to show the Klan in action. For the next hour, we will take a close look at the Ku Klux Klan from the inside out—examine its leadership, its ritual, its secret initiation, its record of violence. First, let us look at Klansmen without their robes.

It is Sunday, the morning after a Ku Klux Klan meeting in Durham, North Carolina. The men being

*A reminder to the reader that this program was televised on September 21, 1965. For a summary of what occurred at the hearings, see the Epilogue.

interviewed are members of the United Klans of America, Knights of the Ku Klux Klan, one of the most exclusive organizations in America. It excludes many Protestants, all Roman Catholics, Jews, Negroes, Spanish Americans, Puerto Ricans, and anyone else who, according to the Ku Klux Klan, is not 100 per cent pure American.

J. ROBERT JONES (*above*):

I don't hate niggers, man. I don't—I don't—I don't associate with niggers. But on the other hand, I don't associate with common white trash or Jews or Catholics if I can help it.

KURALT:

This is the Grand Dragon of the North Carolina realm of the United Klans, J. Robert Jones. Former sailor, bricklayer, lightning-rod salesman, he now re-

K
K
K

portedly rules over more than fifty Klaverns or chapters and their seven thousand dues-paying members.

JONES:

I think the nigger has rights in this country. He should have equal rights, but separate rights. It's worked for a hundred years in the South and I think it will work now. But if you was the nicest fellow in the world and Lyndon Johnson said I had to associate with you every day, I'd tell Lyndon Johnson to go straight to hell because I would not associate with you.

KURALT:

This is the Grand Klonsel, the late Matt Murphy, who until his recent death was chief legal counsel of the United Klans. His favorite targets were the Negroes, the Jews, the Federal Reserve System, and international bankers.

MURPHY:

I had made speeches before the United Klans of America and they were the only organization that ever went on record, after I had talked for two solid hours, on the viciousness of the Federal Reserve Corporation and how it has bilked the taxpayers and the American citizens out of all their money and that Great Britain has removed the bank from the international bankers and their bank is back under the Crown.

KURALT:

This is a Night-hawk of the United Klans in North

Matt Murphy (right) *with a Night-hawk of the United Klans.*

Carolina. A Night-hawk is responsible for the security of a Klavern.

REPORTER:

Why did you join the Klan?

NIGHT-HAWK:

Well, I've got a wife, five kids, and I think that's enough reason. I want them to be—have a country to raise, be raised up in like I was. I wasn't forced to go to school with niggers. I wasn't forced to eat with them. And I want them to have at least the right that I had.

KURALT:

Wherever Jones goes, Mr. Outlaw, the Grand Klex-

K
K
K

ter or guard, is at his side. Also present are the three defendants indicted for the killing of Mrs. Liuzzo: Eugene Thomas, William Eaton, and Collie Leroy Wilkins. These men had little to say. They preferred listening to their counsel, Matt Murphy, Jr.

MURPHY:

I read in my history books that the Negro man, the Negro race was an inferior race. And that was the history

W. O. Eaton (right) *with Mr. Outlaw, Grand Klexter of the North Carolina realm.*

(Left to right) *Klansman, J. Robert Jones, Eugene Thomas, and Collie Leroy Wilkins.*

that was taught me when I was in school. And that hasn't been too long ago.

JONES:

They always have been. They always will be.

REPORTER:

Well, where do you think the money is coming from behind the civil rights movement?

JONES:

From the Communist party. From the Zionist, Christ-killing Jews. And I say Christ-killing Jews because they have not been affluent since they—since they crucified Christ and their relatives can be traced back to the ones that's running in the streets today.

K
K
K

REPORTER:

What about the role of the Catholics in this, Mr. Jones?

JONES:

The reason the Catholic cannot get in this organization, his first allegiance is not to the United States of America, his first allegiance is to the Pope. They believe that the Church should rule the government with the Pope at the head. And if they're right, there's a bunch of people in this country who are wrong.

Let me say this. We have never had a drop of blood spilled between a white man and a black one in any town in North Carolina that we had the Klan organized. And we're doing our best to keep down trouble. But my people are—everybody in this country is organized with the exception of the white Protestant gentile. Your niggers have your Knights—your NAACP and CORE, along with your sorry white trash. You've got B'nai B'rith for your Jewish people. Your Knights of Columbus, which is a secret fraternal order, as they say, and nobody's ever talked about investigating that, which they should in here. But the white Protestant gentile, the only hope and the only salvation that they have left in this United States today, is the United Klans of America, Incorporated. We've saved the South twice—or the Klan has—and it looks like we're going to just have to do it again.

KURALT:

One important Ku Klux Klan official was not at

this meeting, the Klan Kludd or chaplain. But there was a Kludd in action the night before.

ROY WOODLE (*below*):

You got a bunch of people standing right over here with their cameras and their news things. Half of them ain't got enough backbone to get them a job and go to work, but there might be some good ones in the crowd. I want to tell you fellers—I, I'm just telling you, you fellows right over here—they'll print half of the story. They ain't got enough backbone to tell the truth. So

K
K
K

anybody that lies with the devil, you're going to die and go to hell without God. If all you FBI agents want to check the Klan and investigate them, I live on 209 Mendota Avenue, Lexington, North Carolina, and my name is Roy Woodle and I'm not ashamed to be a Klansman. Amen.

KURALT:

This is the Klan Kludd in action, the preacher, evangelist, the hell-fire speaker, the rabble-rouser. He entertains with a mixture of comedy and Christianity, but, above all, he preaches racial hatred.

WOODLE:

Now do you think the children is brought up to mix the black and white together? Do you know your horse won't mix with your cow, your dog won't mix with your hog? And you tell me white people has got a mind and can't think no clearer than that? Listen, friend, we need to turn to God. We need to wake up with God. We had forefathers died to give us freedom. Our forefathers walked barefooted in the snow and fought and died to give us freedom. And now here we sit back because we got a dictator in the White House a-dictating and you sending your money down now to pay it and ain't willing to stand up and be counted like a man or a woman. It takes a man to stand and be a man. Anybody can go down to niggertown and commit adultery with a nigger, but it takes a Christian, a man, to stand for God.

Let me call you farmers to attention to a few things.

You've raised hogs and you know when those hogs has a gang of little pigs, she'll try to protect them. You'll know the dog. When they have a gang of pups, they'll try to protect them. And you tell me you got a gang of white children running around in your yard and you're going to stand by and see them sold out to a bunch of niggers. God help you to wake up and try to do what God will

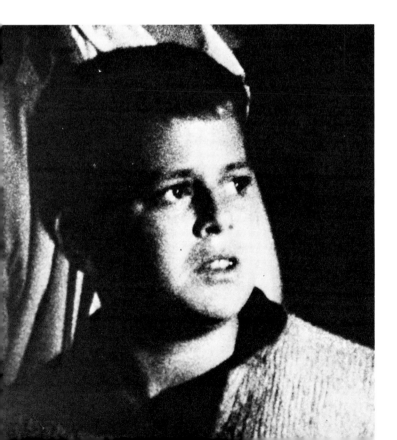

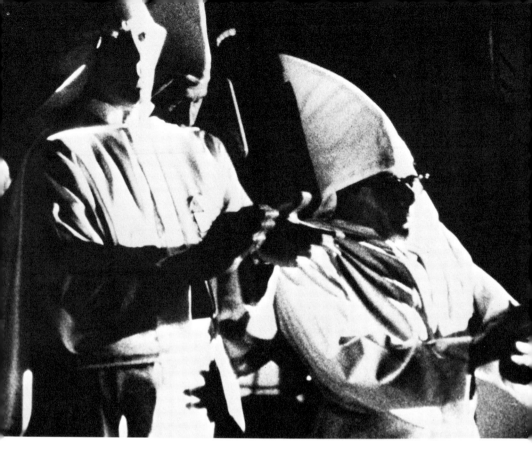

have you do. Protect your own. Act like a decent person. And then if you don't want to do that, don't be a half-hazard hypocrite, don't be one-sided, go into nigger-town and forget about it.

Kuralt:

The Klan was born a hundred years ago in Pulaski, Tennessee, as a six-member social club. But six years later the Klan had a half a million members and the burning cross, the Klan trademark, became a symbol of the violence it used to keep the newly freed Negroes in their place.

In 1915 D. W. Griffith produced and directed what has been called the first great feature-length motion picture, *The Birth of a Nation*, whose subject was the

Ku Klux Klan. Today this film, made fifty years ago, is still shown to Klansmen as the classic example of what other generations of Southerners did to protect white supremacy.

In *The Birth of a Nation* a chance witnessing of two

KILLIAM SHOWS, INC., from *The Birth of a Nation*

white children under a bedsheet scaring a group of Negro children is depicted as the birth of the idea for the Klan. The idea is successful. Robed and masked Klansmen are able to frighten the Negroes. In a fight, the Negro sought for scaring a white girl and causing her to jump from a cliff to her death kills a white man. Captured, the killer is taken into the woods and put on trial. The Klan passes judgment. The culprit is killed and his body deposited at the door of the Lieutenant Governor.

In the same year *The Birth of a Nation* was first released, a new leader rose to head the Klan. William Joseph Simmons, one-time salesman of ladies' garters, led his followers up Stone Mountain in Georgia for the first initiation ceremony of the reincarnated Klan. Simmons added something new to the Klan uniform—a

KILLIAM SHOWS, INC., from *The Birth of a Nation*

stylized face mask, which he alone could wear. He also insisted the Klan operate in total secrecy. The Klan's sinister power grew as new recruits joined, some through coercion, and as its clandestine activities increased. In the first fourteen months after World War I, seventy Negroes were lynched, fourteen burned.

In 1922 Imperial Wizard Simmons could not overcome intra-Klan difficulties and was replaced by a dentist from Dallas, Dr. Hiram Evans, who inherited a depleted treasury from Simmons as well as his title of Imperial Wizard. In 1923 Evans established headquarters in Washington to be closer to Congress, the Klan's next target.

K K K

Dr. Hiram Evans.

The Klan was so powerful in Oregon in 1923 that it was able to elect the President of the State Senate and the Speaker of the House. In Ohio, Klan-supported candidates became mayors of Toledo, Akron, Columbus, and other cities. At the National Democratic convention in New York in 1924, it is estimated that at least 350 delegates were Klansmen and they were responsible for the defeat of Governor Alfred Smith as the Democratic nominee.

By 1925 the Ku Klux Klan was big business. Almost six million Americans now belonged to the Klan and the organization was grossing $75 million a year. Some forty thousand Klansmen and Klanswomen crowded into Washington on August 8, 1925, to parade down Pennsylvania Avenue. To help the Klan coffers, a flag was used to catch money thrown in by spectators.

In the 1920's the Imperial Wizard of Indiana, David C. Stephenson, was indicted on charges of assault and battery, rape, mayhem, kidnaping, and murder, and was found guilty. This scandal caused a sharp drop in Klan membership.

In 1940 there was a mild flirtation between the German-American Bund, the believers in the master race, and the Ku Klux Klan, the believers in the supremacy of the white race. They joined up in a rally at Camp Nordland, New Jersey. Twenty-five years later there is evidence that Klan-Nazi friendship is being revived. In 1965, in Houston, Texas, Jerald Walraven, claiming membership in the United Klans, Knights of the Ku Klux Klan, was interviewed by Radio Station KTRH and was paid by check for his appearance. When the canceled check was returned to the radio station, it had been endorsed by Lincoln Rockwell, head of the American Nazi Party, with a swastika stamped beneath his signature.

Members of the New Jersey KKK appear in 1940 with August Klapproot (right), *regional leader of the German-American Bund.*

James A. Colescott.

In 1944 Imperial Wizard Dr. James H. Colescott received a bill from the U. S. Collector of Internal Revenue for $685,000 for the Klan's back taxes. Unable to pay, Dr. Colescott disbanded the Klan. But four years later, Colescott's former partner, Dr. Samuel Green, reactivated the Klan and many new converts were initiated into Klandom, motivated by a desire to keep the Negro in his place. At a rally in Macon, Georgia, Imperial Wizard Green defended the new Klan.

GREEN:

We don't hate the Negro. God made him black and He made us white and you will find this laid out in the

K
K
K

Eleventh Chapter of Genesis, in which He segregated the races. And we, knowing that for five thousand years the white man has been the supreme race, we, the Knights of the Ku Klux Klan, intend to keep it the white race.

Dr. Samuel Green.

KURALT:

Today the organization differs from the past in that Klansmen are willing to appear in their robes and hoods in daylight. With the advent of the civil rights struggle, the Klan has become more militant. Some groups have paramilitary units, such as this one in North Carolina. Grand Dragon Jones's security guards are trained to take care of anything that might happen at Klan rallies.

The Klan also sponsors softball teams. Since softball can't be played in robes, KKK letters appear on the uniform to remind the spectators that this team is made up of 100 per cent pure white American Protestant ball players.

Sometimes Klansmen engage in more bizarre sport. The letters KKK were carved with a pen knife on the chest and stomach of a man in Houston, Texas, after he had been hanged by his knees from an oak tree and flogged with a chain.

The Attorney General of Alabama, Richmond Flowers, told us:

FLOWERS:

The Klan to me is a group primarily of thugs that would use the civil rights issue to foster an organization

HEARST METROTONE NEWS

Richmond Flowers.

or a Klan, as they are, and will take the law into their own hands. They have become more or less—more or less their own police power. They are a police group within themselves, dedicated to defiance of law and violence. They are, as I have expressed it before, they are a hooded bunch of killers and nightriders and floggers that this nation and this state has no use for whatsoever.

KURALT:

The strength of the Ku Klux Klan is difficult to estimate. Among its many secrets is the actual membership total. Students of Klan affairs say there are at least thirty thousand to fifty thousand active members. But there are probably as many as a million or more Americans who are strongly sympathetic to the aims of the Klan and who, if pushed to a decision, would join the

Klan. When a 100 per cent pure white American citizen applies for membership, his application is carefully checked. If accepted, he can then leave what the Klan calls the "alien world" and become a member of the Invisible Empire.

For the first time in Klan history, CBS News cameras filmed part of a secret initiation ceremony at a Klavern in Georgia. Filming had to be done with available light and the only parts of the ritual we could not film were the secret handshake, the password by which Klansmen identify themselves to each other, and the secret oath of allegiance to the Imperial Authority of the Klan. The ceremony began with a pledge.

KLANSMEN:

For my country and my Klan, our fellow Klansmen and our home, I pledge allegiance to the flag of the United States of America and to the Republic for which it stands, one nation, under God, indivisible, with liberty and justice for all.

KURALT:

Five initiates appeared before an Exalted Cyclops, a Klokard, Kludd, and Kligrapp, corresponding to a president, lecturer, chaplain, and secretary. The men were presented by the Klokard and they had been checked out by the Klokann or investigating committee.

On a makeshift altar before an electrified cross are placed a sword, representing ancestral courage, and a

flag, the emblem of pure patriotism. An open Bible is laid on the flag. A glass of water, which is used to consecrate the initiates, completes the symbolic array. A Klarogo or inner guard sits at the door. On the other side is a Klexter or outer guard. The Klokard and two assistants report to the Exalted Cyclops.

KLOKARD:

Your Excellency, sir, five men in waiting have equally and duly qualified in our Klavern during and through the mysticating quest for citizenship in the Invisible Empire, United Klans, Knights of the Ku Klux Klan.

CYCLOPS:

Faithful Klokard, you and your assistants will resume your stations.

KLOKARD:

We have, your honor. Follow me and be proven.

KLAROGO:

Forward march. Halt. You will stand in silence and take heed to the Klansman's prayer.

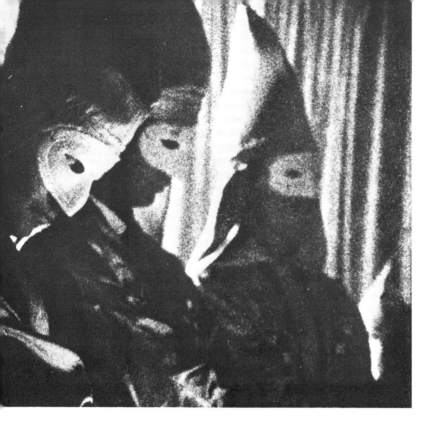

KLUDD:
God, give us Men! . . .
Men who can stand before a demagogue
And damn his treacherous flattery . . .
Tall men, sun-crowned, who live above the fog
In public duty and in private thinking;
For while the rabble, with their thumb-worn creeds,
Their large professions and their little deeds,
Mingle in selfish strife, lo! Freedom weeps,
Wrong rules the land and waiting justice sleeps.
God, give us Men!
NIGHT-HAWK:
Right face. Halt. Left face. Left face.
KURALT:
This is the "eyes of scrutiny" part of the initiation
ceremony. Klan members pass by the initiates for one
last searching look.

CYCLOPS:
You may pass on.

NIGHT-HAWK:
Right face. Forward march.

KURALT:
In this room the initiates swear allegiance to the Klan above all things. The secrecy and ritual of these meetings, which seem almost laughable to the outsider,

K
K
K

have a grimly serious purpose. Because of its secrecy, the Klan can hold sway over a community. When men are initiated into Klandom, in rituals such as this one, their neighbors will not know they have become Klansmen. If some of the initiates are policemen or sheriffs' deputies, their fellow officers will not know. If they are jurors, their fellow jurors will not know. Under the cloak of this secrecy, the Klan can take over positions of influence and power.

KLUDD:

I beseech you therefore, brethren, by the mercies of God that you present your body as a living sacrifice. Be ye transformed by the renewing of your mind that you may prove what is that good and acceptable in perfect will of God. We recognize our relations to the Government of the United States of America, the supremacy of its Constitution, the Union of States thereon, and the constitutional laws thereof. And we shall ever be true and faithfully maintain white supremacy and will strenuously oppose any compromise thereof in any and all things. Are you a native-born, white, gentile, American citizen?

INITIATES:

Yes.

KLUDD:

Do you believe in the tenets of the Christian religion?

INITIATES:

Yes.

KLUDD:

Do you esteem the United States of America and its institutions above any other government, civil, political, or ecclesiastical, in the whole world?

INITIATES:

Yes.

CYCLOPS:

Kneel on your right knee. Klansmen, one and all, let us pray. Sirs, you may now rise. Sirs, you are no longer aliens or strangers among us, but are citizens with us. And assuming that you haven't foresworn falsely or deceitfully in assuming your oath and now on behalf of all Klansmen assembled, welcome you to citizenship in The Invisible Empire, Knights of the Ku Klux Klan.

KURALT:

The five new Klansmen are no longer part of the "alien world." Now they are members of The Invisible

K
K
K

Empire, entitled to wear the robe and the hood, the proud possessors of the secret handshake and the secret password. And now they can attend Klavern meetings and Klan rallies, such as this one in Dunn, North Carolina.

A Klan rally has many elements of a carnival. It's an outing for the family. Children start attending these outdoor meetings at an early age. Robes for the youngsters are made by mothers and follow the pattern of adult robes. Rallies always have entertainers and their

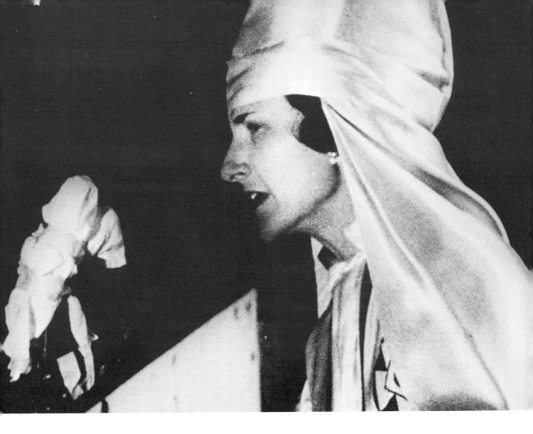

material is Klan-tailored for the audience. This entertainer recites a poem:

KLANSWOMAN:

"The Saddest Story Ever Told."

When a white girl marries a Negro,
Her sun of light goes down
And glaring spots of sin
Appear on her wedding gown.

And white and black men stand aghast
While viewing this strange role
And mutter, "They will wreck themselves
And damn each other's soul."

Three days and nights she felt black lips
Pressed smug against her own

And on the fourth her troubled soul
Let out a frightened groan.

And so I stagger through my days
Far from God's love and grace,
Till now I know no black man lives
Can take a white man's place.

Thank you.

KURALT:
The featured speaker is usually a well-known per-
sonality. At this rally it was the late Matt Murphy, Jr.,
Imperial Klonsel or chief legal counsel of the United
Klans.

MURPHY:
And I'll tell you this, and go to your Congressman,
ask him what to do, and tell him what to do because

they're about to pass a bill up there that if you strike a
civil rights worker, it's a federal offense and they'll haul
you before a federal court and take you to the most
favorable county they can find and cut your head off if
they can. And when I say cut your head off, I mean
they'll send you to the federal penitentiary. That's the
way they're doing it. That's the way they call the shots.
So for God's sake, get your Congressman and if he
doesn't do it, elect somebody that will fight such a bill
as that.

W. O. Eaton.

KURALT:

As extra added attraction, Matt Murphy introduced the three men indicted for the murder of civil
rights worker, Mrs. Viola Liuzzo.

MURPHY:

Mr. W. O. Eaton. Mr. Eugene Thomas. And the
boy who stood under the battle guns, Collie Leroy
Wilkins.

KURALT:

And befitting the occasion of a Ku Klux Klan rally,

Collie Leroy Wilkins.

W. O. Eaton, Eugene Thomas, and Collie Leroy Wilkins sign autographs at Klan rally.

the three men were beseiged by autograph hunters and they willingly obliged.

Klan members accused of crimes must be defended. Their Klonsels or attorneys must be paid. In addition, money is required for operating expenses and leaders' salaries, which run as high as $1,500 a month. The Invisible Empire needs a treasury. But where the money comes from and how much is a secret. What is known is that initiation fees are between ten and twenty-five dollars, and yearly dues for assessments range from three to fifteen dollars. A conservative estimate is that the Klan is a million-dollar-a-year enterprise. The money comes from initiation fees, dues, robe and hood sales, individual contributions, and from what can be raised by a Klan Kludd at a rally.

KLUDD:

There might be a businessman that's prosperous and you can afford to give a thousand. You can afford to pay one of the men's salary. There might be a businessman. There is. There may be some company that can

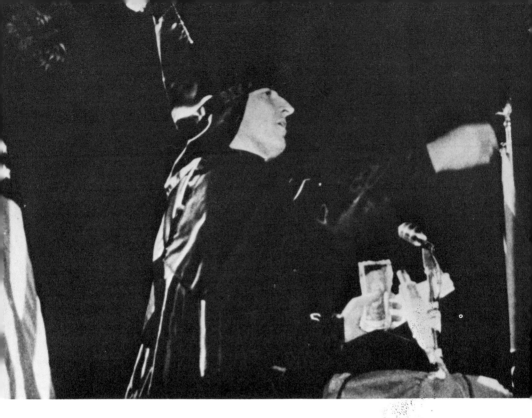

write a check for one man's year's salary to do nothing but set up units throughout North Carolina. Whatever you have, ten dollars, five dollars, walk down with it. Will you do that? Is there others? You know, we ought to be able tonight, we ought tonight to be able to come way on up the ladder. We're going to count this just as soon as I leave the platform and let you know how much there is.

KURALT:

The men and women in robes receive torches and the parade around the Kuklos or circle begins. This scene—seven hundred robed and hooded men marching around a burning cross—took place in the United States in 1965.

Klan leaders are sensitive about the reputation the Klan has for intimidation and violence. In an attempt to erase this image, they have adopted a new policy which, in effect, says: "Look at us. We are a fraternal organiza-

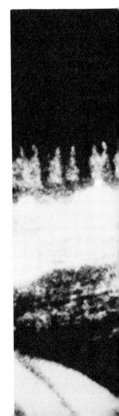

tion. We have nothing to hide." Imperial Wizards and Grand Dragons no longer avoid the press. Klan leaders sport crew cuts, button-down collars, and well-tailored suits. The most publicized and best-organized Klan leader is Imperial Wizard Robert Shelton of the United Klans, Knights of the KKK. Shelton spends much of his time in his Tuscaloosa, Alabama, office, constantly listening to tape recordings of Martin Luther King, Jr., while he examines pictures of civil rights demonstrators. Those he can identify are circled and filed. Shelton explains why.

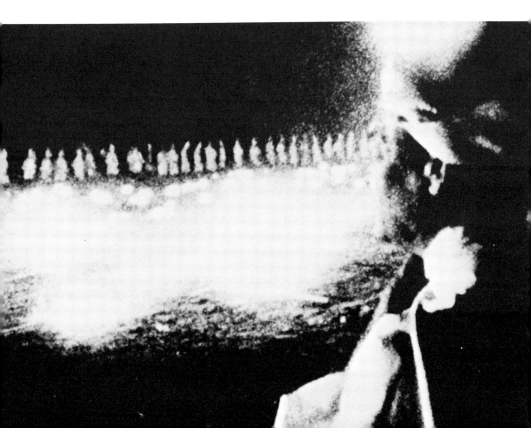

Robert Shelton (*above*):

We have a division in our organization called the KBI, the Klan Bureau of Investigation. And I might add, it is pretty effective. We are able to uncover a lot of evidence that other departments might miss.

Kuralt:

It is estimated that Imperial Wizard Shelton is the highest-paid officer in Klandom. He has a private airplane, a limousine, and he travels constantly. As Imperial Wizard, Shelton has several Grand Dragons or State Governors under his command: Grand Dragon of the Georgia realm, Calvin Craig; Grand Dragon of South Carolina, Robert Scoggins; Grand Dragon of Mississippi, E. L. McDaniel; Florida's Grand Dragon, Don Cothran; Grand Dragon of Tennessee, Raymond Anderson.

Calvin Craig.

Robert Scoggins.

E. L. McDaniel.

Don Cothran.

Raymond Anderson.

Klan leaders constantly preach race hatred. Every Klan speaker warns against mongrelization of the races. And hearing this theme of white supremacy repeated over and over again, some Klan members come to believe their status is threatened and commit acts of violence. Immediately Klan officials deny responsibility for the criminal acts of their members. In rare cases in which Klansmen are arrested, the leaders even deny these men are members of their group.

Yet it is known that there are approximately five thousand hard-core members of the Klan who are obsessed and fanatical—fanatical enough to set fires, bomb, dynamite, and even kill. The question is: How can Klan leaders avoid responsibility for violence when they themselves repeatedly whip up their members to action? Go to any Klan meeting, this is what you'll hear:

KLANSMAN:

White man, is this your country or does it belong to the niggers?

VOICE:

White man.

JAMES VENABLE (*below*), IMPERIAL WIZARD, NATIONAL KNIGHTS OF THE KKK:

If you want your daughter, your son to marry a nigger, hold up your hand and let me look you in the eyes, if you're a white man or a white woman in this great nation there.

ROBERT CREEL, GRAND DRAGON, ALABAMA REALM OF THE UNITED KLANS:

"We're on the move." That's what the Negroes are

K
K
K

hollering. "We're on the move. We're on the go. We're going to run the white people down. We're going to kick them in the teeth. We going to take our place in society." I got news for nigger, for you niggers. We're on the move too. I don't believe in segregation. I believe in slavery.

KURALT:

The Klan says it does not advocate intimidation, harassment, or violence, that it is a peaceful organization. Let us take a look at some proven Klan activities.

In the small community of Gray, Georgia, the only movie theater in town permitted Negroes to sit in the balcony. The Klan decided this was not a healthy thing for the white people, and every Friday night fifty carloads of robed Klansmen circled the theater. Today the movie house in Gray, Georgia, is closed—a victory for the Klan.

Further examples of Klan intimidation were uncovered in an injunction lawsuit in the Fifth Circuit Court of Appeals in New Orleans. The hearings revealed that in Bogalusa, Louisiana, sometimes called Klantown, U.S.A., some of the city's estimated thousand Klan members were auxiliary policemen. The City Attorney, who is responsible for prosecuting charges against Klansmen arrested for violence against civil rights workers, was himself identified as a Klansman.

The powerful Bogalusa Klan moved this year against Radio Station WBOX, whose owner was one of a group which invited former Arkansas Congressman Brooks Hays to make a speech in Bogalusa on race relations. Klansmen made hundreds of anonymous phone calls to the station's sponsors. The effect was immediate; 75 per cent of the commercials were canceled. WBOX is still broadcasting, but at a loss.

Although the Klan says it has respect for law and order, there are records of countless crimes which some Klansmen performed for reasons they deemed proper. Judge Daniel Duke (*below*), who has fought the Klan for twenty-five years in Georgia, tells how the Klan administered its own kind of justice.

K
K
K

DANIEL DUKE:

They'd have a—the Klokann Committee, the committee that administered the floggings. One would get on one side of this man, who was doubled up with his wrist handcuffed to his ankles, who had been taken from his home, he thought by a legal warrant, and who had, unknown to him, been reported by someone to be a labor organizer. And they equated that to communism. And then they equated that to race-mixing. And they would usually equate that to say some Jewish person was back of it and a multiplicity of things—anything that appealed to hate, prejudice. They'd take this man and they would beat him unmercifully.

KURALT:

The Ku Klux Klan does not stop at floggings. In 1957 in Birmingham, Alabama, a group of Klansmen

committed the most heinous crime short of murder. As a warning to civil rights leaders, they abducted this man and castrated him.

MAN:

They hit me in the back of the head and told me to lay down and they all grabbed me and stretched me out. One stood on this arm and one stood on this one and caught my leg and spread it apart. Then he got help from the other one and they spread my leg apart. The boss ordered him to "do your work" and they went to cutting on me. When they got through cutting me, they put turpentine on me and said I wouldn't holler—put turpentine on to make it hurt more. I don't believe they're human.

KURALT:

But not only individuals suffer at the hands of the Klan. Sometimes whole cities are victims. In one large city, there is evidence that Klan-inspired violence touched off one of the most vicious racial riots in recent history. The place was St. Augustine, Florida. This Klansman was primarily responsible for what happened.

Reverend Connie Lynch (*above*) is probably the most effective rabble-rouser and preacher of bigotry the Klan has to offer.

LYNCH:

Most people would kill you if you put a Jersey bull in among their white-faced Herefords. They'd shoot you. But to tell me I don't even have the right to fight to protect the white race . . . let these black bucks come in. They said it was going to be settled in the bedroom. Well, I got some news for them. There may be some bedroom cases all right. But when the smoke clears away, there won't be no bedroom cases.

KURALT:

Little Rock; Oxford; Birmingham; Albany, Georgia; Bogalusa, Louisiana—Connie Lynch was there. And when racial violence was predicted for St. Augustine, Florida, Connie Lynch went there too. Negroes were trying to integrate the bathing beaches and the

Florida Advisory Committee to the U. S. Civil Rights Commission warned that the city was becoming a racial "superbomb" with a "short fuse."

WOMAN:

When the police stand up on the corners and hit the white fellers in the stomach with the blackjacks for standing on the corners and the white people going to march through and take it.

KURALT:

The tempo of violence increased rapidly in St.

UPI

Augustine. The Klan paraded in the streets, unmindful of the rain.

LYNCH:

And I'll say this to the stooges that want to take this back to the enemy camp, to the niggers and all their cohorts, that we white people are going to rise up a hundred and forty million strong and . . .

KURALT:

On the night of June 25, 1964, the fuse burned down and the racial bomb exploded. St. Augustine was the scene of a frightening riot. Scores of people were in-

jured, nineteen hospitalized. Connie Lynch had done his work.

LYNCH:

I spoke for the white people. The white people rallied behind it and we kicked the living hell out of the niggers, sent the out-of-town niggers to the hospital and out of the state back to their own home towns where they ought to have been, and the niggers in St. Augustine got quiet and went back over to niggertown where they belong.

KURALT:

These examples of Ku Klux Klan activity are not

K
K
K

unusual. For the past one hundred years, The Invisible Empire, this self-proclaimed second national government, has reserved to itself police authority and the right to correct what it considers wrong. Although some Klansmen have been apprehended and tried for their crimes, the fact remains that the perpetrators of more than 225 bombings and 1,000 acts of racial violence, reprisal, and intimidation in the last ten years have not been arrested. The problem is that law enforcement itself is often in the hands of authorities who either belong to or sympathize with the Ku Klux Klan. The publisher of the *Atlanta Constitution,* Ralph McGill, ex-

plains why citizens are powerless to protest in such situations.

McGILL:

In the small community you too often find that the sheriff is a member or that the deputies are members. And the poor white man, or more particularly the poor Negro in a small community, he well knows that he has no protection at all. The law isn't going to help him because the law is, more often than not, in the Klan or sympathetic with it in the small Southern community.

KURALT:

The Grand Dragon of Georgia, Calvin Craig, confirmed that law enforcement officers are Klansmen.

CRAIG:

We have policemen. We have sheriffs. We have farmers. We have mechanics. And myself, I'm an operating engineer.

KURALT:

One law enforcement officer sympathetic to the Klan, Sheriff Lawrence Rainey of Neshoba County, Mississippi, was charged in the death of civil rights workers Schwerner, Goodman, and Chaney. Recently Sheriff Rainey was introduced at a Klan rally by the Grand Dragon of Mississippi, E. L. McDaniel, and offered a testimonial to members of the Klan.

McDANIEL:

I would like at this time to call Sheriff Lawrence A.

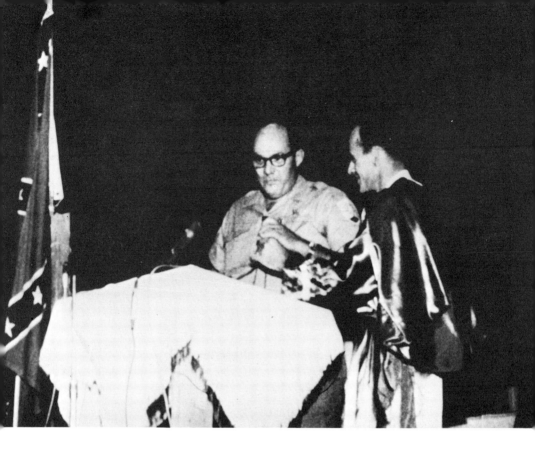

Rainey from Neshoba County to the platform for a statement. Are you proud he's here?

RAINEY:

Thank you.

VOICE:

Where's your Red Man?

RAINEY:

It's in the car. Can't do without that. No, I was just down here. I've been accused by the FBI, by the Klan and everything and so I come down today to see the head man and investigate it and see what there was to it. And I found it so far to be mighty good. They just done a lot of lying about it. I've met some of the best fellows I think there are in Alabama and Mississippi and other places. And I've had to lay some deputies out that's been investigating it and they reported to me a while ago, they'd met some fine people and thought it was a mighty good organization. Thank you.

McDaniel:

Let's give him a hand if you're glad he got on this platform. A true, great, white American.

Kuralt:

The Klan is not a single, strongly organized group. It is composed of splinter groups fighting each other for new members and new territory. On Memorial Day weekend, 1965, Robert Shelton's chief rival, James Venable, head of the National Knights of the KKK, took his Klan north to a site twenty-five miles from Cincinnati, Ohio. Both Venable and Shelton believe the whites in the North, worried about Negro civil rights demands in their own communities, are ready to embrace the Klan. This was the first open Klan rally in Ohio in more than thirty years. The fact that the Klan is getting bolder was demonstrated by the site which was selected, right alongside superhighway 75. Klan robes, many of which had been stored away for years, were put out for an airing. Since the building of a cross for the Klan ritual requires skill, out-of-staters volunteered to hammer the cross pieces, wrap the burlap carefully, and then soak their handiwork with a mixture of gasoline and motor oil—a half gallon of gasoline and five pounds of oil for every foot of the cross.

Men:

This side. Look out. All right. Hold it. Hey, fellow, get off those wires.

KURALT:

The Klan added a new touch to attract crowds, a sky-diving show with parachute jumpers releasing Klan flags and then landing on Klan-blessed land.

The northernmost penetration of the Klan took place in 1965 near Cleveland, Ohio. All cars headed for the rally were searched for weapons, and police confiscated high-powered rifles, shotguns, and pistols. There were the usual preparations, including the raising of the cross. At a nearby restaurant, men lined up to get applications for membership in Imperial Wizard Venable's Knights of the Ku Klux Klan. That evening twenty-five men and women, kept at a safe distance, picketed the meeting. The burning of the cross was the high point of this rally, only twenty-one miles from Cleveland.

Does The Invisible Empire have a right to continue its activities either in the North or the South? In our democracy, freedom of speech must be accorded this organization. Klansmen have a right to meet and wear uniforms. If the Klan is a fraternal order, it should enjoy the privileges of other orders. But the truth is that

among all such organizations, only the Klan has a history of violence.

Lawmakers have not ignored the Klan: Twenty-two states have passed laws prohibiting the wearing of masks in public and fifty-two southern communities have outlawed masks and cross burnings. But even these laws have been ineffective. Klansmen can still legally wear masks and burn crosses on private property. They still intimidate and harass citizens.

Now the office of the Attorney General is working on new anti-Klan legislation for submission to Congress. Attorney General Katzenbach (*above*) was asked what form this legislation might take.

KATZENBACH:

Well, I think it could take a number of forms. One would be to follow the analogy with respect to the Com-

munist party and to seek full disclosure of their membership and a listing of the Klan and its members and its
officers as a sort of glare of publicity. Another approach,
perhaps a better approach, would be to follow the pattern of the existing laws, but to expand their scope of
federal jurisdiction under them and to increase the
penalties under them so that the federal government
could get a more deep involvement.

KURALT:

We've put up with the Klan for a hundred years
in this country. How long is it going to take for us to
see the end of the Klan?

KATZENBACH:

I don't know when we'll see the end of the Klan. I
think the end of the Klan as any kind of an effective
organization of any sort at all is within sight. I doubt
that the Klan is going to be a very effective force any-
where ten years from now.

KURALT:

Today still another investigation of the Klan is
being conducted in Washington by the House Un-
American Activities Committee. The Committee has
issued more than two hundred subpoenas. The Chairman is Representative Edwin Willis of Louisiana.

WILLIS:

It is certainly a clear and present danger to communities and to areas within which they operate.
There's no question about it. It's perilous. It's terroristic.

Edwin Willis.

Now, I wouldn't want to dignify them into believing that they're a clear and present danger to our Government of the United States. I hope we can extinguish the flame before the fire reaches such proportions.

KURALT:

One of the subcommittee members, Representative Charles Weltner of Georgia, was asked how the Klan could be curbed.

WELTNER:

One of the reasons it's difficult to convict a Klansman is because nobody knows who else is a Klansman. Nobody knows whether jurors are Klansmen. They're under mandate to lie about their Klan activity when they're examined. That's a mandate higher than the oath that is required of all jurors. One of the reasons it's hard to convict Klansmen is because of the secrecy, the terror, the unknown quantity, the mystery of the

Charles L. Weltner.

Klan. Now when we strip this organization of those elements, then the Klan becomes a group of small, willful men who have devoted their activities to hatred and they are simply not going to be accepted for what they really are when the people know what they really are.

WILLIS:

I predict that there's going to be weeping and wailing and gnashing of teeth. And all the protestations about how great and how dedicated the Klansmen are and how attached they are to Christianity—I'm afraid a a few little balloons are going to be bursted before this thing is over.

KURALT:

The impending Committee hearings will focus the national spotlight on the Ku Klux Klan and it is possible that part of The Invisible Empire may become visible. Defections have been noted. Earlier in this program we

showed Reverend Roy Woodle, a Klan Kludd, in action.
A few days ago, Woodle quit the United Klans, Incor-
porated. Last week at his home near Lexington, North
Carolina, we asked him why.

WOODLE:

Well, if people would just check the record and see
just now what, who is leading the Klan and what are
they and what they stand for—that would be a logical question. So take any individual, what if he be in the
Klan or out, check the leadership. Say, for example, we
have people was painter-contractors. Far as I know,
failures. We have people was insurance agencies. Far
as I know, failures. We have people was concrete business. Far as I know, failures. And such as that—just
failed out and flunked out. Come promote leadership
and just lost out everything they had and then, well,

when they couldn't find nothing else to do, the fellows said they made them a Klan leader.

Take, for instance, you make a man a security guard and pin a little old bar or something on him, he thinks he's a big wheel and a deal and, therefore, he'll follow it till he spend all of his money every weekend

for gas, run up and down the road right—just that he can get out there and strut with them bars on, think he's a big shot of some kind. If he go back home and check his home, no doubt he wouldn't have no decent food in his house to eat.

KURALT:

Is there immorality in the Klan, un-Christian kind of activity?

WOODLE:

Now if a man will go to a Klan rally professing to be a preacher—let me put emphasis on that, professing to be a preacher—gets up and bows his head and says he's praying to the Lord for people to help give and then plant a man out in the crowd with a hundred-dollar bill, one with a fifty, and say: "Now who will give a hundred dollars?" and ask it, then that man will come forth and try to bewitch somebody else to come. Now that's deceiving the people.

KURALT:

Do some of the Klan leaders misuse the people's money?

WOODLE:

If he's going to promote leadership, why ride around in a big car, telephone in it, jump out at rallies, which you fellows know does—everybody does—and gets up on the platform, makes his speech, holds his rally, they take up the money, then they're off. And they have no more leadership from there. The next year

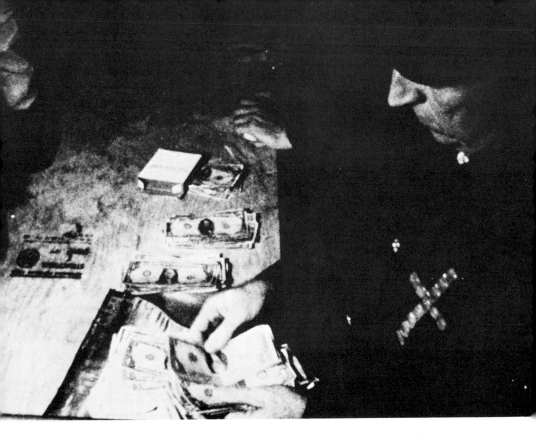

they'll come back with the same thing: another rally, big Cadillac, a big speech, and away again.

KURALT:

At every Klan meeting, Reverend Woodle, they go around and collect money. What happens to that money? Where does it go?

WOODLE:

Well, far as we know, it all finds its way in the pockets of the leaders. Now if you know where any else, but I don't myself as an individual. I just couldn't tell you. Now we know that they do take up money every rally. Now we know that. The news knows it. Everybody there knows it. They pass the buckets around and they do take up money. But far as we know, that's the end of it. We don't have no record or nothing else, as far as I know now. Somebody else may

K
K
K

know something I don't know. But all we know is people rides around, lives in their motels, drives their Cadillacs, eats their rib-eye steaks, and laughs at the poor people as they go by.

KURALT:

When the House Un-American Activities Committee begins its hearings, the confrontation between committee members and Klan leaders and followers should provide interesting answers. If an Imperial Wizard is asked at these hearings to name members of his Klan group who may be judges, police chiefs, and legislators, what will happen? Will he do so or will he choose to plead the Fifth Amendment? What will happen when a Klan Kludd is asked where the money he collects at a rally ends up? What will the array of Kleagles and Kladds and Kludds say when they are asked about the reports of secret Klan bank accounts in the names of fish and game clubs in the South? And how does a check to a Klansman end up in the accounts of the Nazi party? What will happen when a Grand Dragon is asked to give the names of Klansmen who may have participated in acts of racial violence? What will the traveling ministers of the Klan faith say if they are asked how race riots start? Will they plead the Fifth Amendment? And if certain sheriffs are asked under oath whether they are Klan members and whether they know the details of unpunished crimes, how will they answer?

K
K
K

Those House Committee hearings on the Klan begin next month. The Attorney General's recommendations for new laws may be expected by the end of the year. Washington is moving against the Klan. But whatever happens to the Ku Klux Klan will not, finally, happen in Washington. It will happen in those small towns of the South whose natural spirit of generosity and justice have been damped and whose leaders have fallen silent. If the Klan prospers, it will draw its strength from such communities. If the Klan falls, it will be because one man, and then another in such places, have made up their own minds that a free society cannot coexist with an Invisible Empire.

FOR months on Capitol Hill a parade of witnesses trooped into the ornate hearing room with the chandeliers, marble columns, and velvet draperies. The setting was familiar. Once again, the House Un-American Activities Committee was conducting a heralded investigation, and once again the corridors were filled with an army of newsmen, with banks of television cameras and floodlights, with congressmen bearing prepared statements for the press, and with the casual and the curious who flock to the place of the latest sensation.

The sensation this time had an irresistibly piquant twist; this time the Un-American Activities Committee was taking on the Ku Klux Klan. Day after day Wizards and Dragons, Kludds and Klabees took the stand—and immediately took the Fifth Amendment. They would not answer questions; they would not produce records. After months, the hearings sputtered and ended without even a formal committee report. There was much talk of legislation growing out of the investigation. Nothing happened. At this writing, in March 1967, not a single bill has been introduced to curb the KKK.

In truth, the committee's investigation of the Klan demonstrated little that was new, and it had no measurable impact in decreasing the Klan's influence. Indeed, it could be argued that the hearings and the attendant publicity helped build membership. In the end, the vaunted investigation provided only a vivid spectacle of one American anachronism examining another American anachronism.

There was, however, one specific result. The House of Representatives, by a tally of 344–28, voted to cite seven Klan officials for contempt of Congress for their refusal to produce records and other documents. On September 14, 1966, Robert M. Shelton the dour Imperial Wizard and ranking Klansman in the country, was convicted on the contempt of Congress charge after a trial in the U.S. District Court in Washington, D.C. Shelton was sentenced to a year in prison and fined $1,000. He has appealed, and remains free at this date. The other Klan officials, Marshall R. Korengay of Virginia; J. R. Jones of North Carolina; Robert E. Scoggins of South Carolina; Calvin F. Craig of Georgia; George F. Dorsett, and Robert Hudgins, have not been tried yet. All of them remain as active in the Klan as in the past.

Shelton, speaking for them all in his customarily contemptuous manner, has pledged that the Klan will continue to fight. "It will take more than the federal bureaucracy to keep us down," he said. And he also sneeringly claims that President Johnson's opposition has granted the KKK more popularity. Unfortunately, he may well be right.

Bringing the Klan to justice in other celebrated southern jury cases has remained equally frustrating.

Two of the three Klansmen, Collie Leroy Wilkins and Eugene Thomas, charged with murdering Mrs. Viola Liuzzo have been acquitted. The third, William Orville Eaton, died of a heart attack before he could be brought to trial. In the Lemuel A. Penn murder case in Georgia, two Klansmen were quickly acquitted. But later they were arrested on lesser charges—of conspiring to violate Penn's civil rights. This time, in the summer of 1966, they were convicted and sentenced to a maximum of ten years. Four fellow Klansmen, tried on the same charges with them, were acquitted. In March 1967 the murder case of the three civil rights workers near Philadelphia, Mississippi—Michael Schwerner, Andrew Goodman, and James Chaney—was reopened. Nineteen men, including Sheriff Lawrence Rainey and his deputy, Cecil Price, were indicted for that crime. Earlier charges against them had been thrown out on legal technicalities. All of those charged were members of the Klan, the FBI stated.

The administration of justice is only the most visible of the problems in connection with the Klan. Even more important are the community attitudes which tacitly condone or permit the Klan to flourish. The present evidence of the racial climate offers slight hope for the immediate future. If anything, racial attitudes have hardened across the country. In the Deep South, particularly, the voice of the moderate has been even further stilled.

In Bogalusa, Louisiana, Ralph Blumberg, the radio station manager who courageously fought the Klan, finally was driven out of the city. He now lives with his family in St. Louis. In Atlanta, Charles Longstreet Weltner, the grandson of a Confederate general and the young congressman who as much as anyone was responsible for setting off the congressional investigation of the Klan, withdrew from the political scene rather than support Lester G. Maddox, the arch-segregationist governor of Georgia. "I cannot compromise with hate," Weltner said, in a memorable farewell to active politics.

But hate is still a factor in his region, and so is the Ku Klux Klan.

As only one of several discouraging recent signs, it was estimated early in 1967 that KKK membership had increased by about twenty thousand during 1966. The Anti-Defamation League attributed the growth to so-called "white backlash" as an outgrowth of racial fear and violence in both North and South. And, as I write this, today's newspaper carries a report from the Virginia Human Relations Commission warning that "white extremists have launched a vicious campaign of terror," with accompanying cross burnings, throughout the Old Dominion—a state which has been relatively free of racial violence.

The reports of continued Klan growth and influence must be comforting to such as Robert Shelton; they bear out his previous forecasts. As he once said to me in a long interview in his Alabama office, "There was a Klan yesterday, there's a Klan today, and there'll be a Klan tomorrow."

In the long perspective of that tomorrow, the final outcome is clear: the Klan will be an ugly memory. Yet today, as the Klan fights what may well be its last long battle in the midst of an emotional civil rights movement, the South and the nation are in for more trouble.

HAYNES JOHNSON

A KLAN GLOSSARY

AYAK	(The Challenge) "Are you a Klansman?"
AKIA	(The Password) "A Klansman I am."
IMPERIAL WIZARD	Chief of the Invisible Empire
GRAND DRAGON	Head of a realm, usually a state
TITAN	Head of a province, usually a Congressional District
CYCLOPS	Head of a Klavern
KLALIFF	Vice President of a Klavern
KLIGRAPP	Secretary
KLABEE	Treasurer
KLUDD	Chaplain
KLOKARD	Lecturer
KLEAGLE	Organizer
KLONSEL	Supreme legal counsel
KLEXTER	An official
KLAROGO	An official
KLOKAN	An official
KLORAN	The Klan Bible
KLAVERN	Klan den or chapter
KLANKRAFT	Practices and beliefs of the Klan
KLONVOCATION	The Imperial Legislature
KLONCILIUM	The Klonvocation's advisory group
KLONKAVE	Monthly meeting
KLORERO	State meeting
KLECTOKEN	Initiation fee

K
K
K

INVISIBLE EMPIRE
The universal geographical jurisdiction of the Klan

KNOCK-OFF SQUADS
The Klan's "action groups," also known as "Holy Terrors"; these are the squads that bomb, flog, tar and feather, abduct, raid, and murder

NIGHT-HAWK
Chief investigator; most Klans now have a KBI—Klan Bureau of Investigation—made up of Klansmen who spy on the enemy

DAVID LOWE

David Lowe was one of television's leading producers of informational broadcasts. His last work, CBS Reports *Ku Klux Klan: The Invisible Empire*, was broadcast only a few days before Mr. Lowe's death on September 25, 1965, at the age of fifty-two.

David Lowe was a broadcast journalist in the best of the Murrow tradition. The list of his broadcasts are his finest eulogy—*Harvest of Shame*, *Who Speaks for Birmingham?*, *Sabotage in South Africa*, *Abortion and the Law*, *Ku Klux Klan: The Invisible Empire*.

Before joining CBS Reports, Mr. Lowe was Executive Producer for NBC's National Education Project. He had also held the post of Director of News, Public Affairs, and Special Events for the Dumont Television Network, and had acted as Executive Program Consultant for England's Granada Television Network.

Among other honors, *Ku Klux Klan: The Invisible Empire*, for which Palmer Williams was Executive Producer, received a Peabody award in 1966 and won first prize in the sociological category at the seventh competition of the Festival dei Popoli at Florence, Italy. David Lowe, as producer and writer, won a posthumous Emmy award for outstanding achievement in news and documentaries. The award was accepted by Mr. Lowe's widow, columnist Harriet Van Horne.

HAYNES JOHNSON

Haynes Bonner Johnson, special assignments reporter for *The Washington Evening Star,* was awarded the Pulitzer Prize for distinguished national reporting in 1966. He was cited for his coverage "of the civil rights conflict centered about Selma, Alabama, and particularly his reporting of its aftermath." A part of that "aftermath" included a personal investigation of the activities of the Ku Klux Klan in the Deep South.

Mr. Johnson was born in 1931 in New York City. After graduating from the University of Missouri's journalism school, he spent three years in the service and then earned a master's degree in American history from the University of Wisconsin. He joined *The Washington Star* in 1957, and has been honored for his reporting on three occasions by the Washington Newspaper Guild.

Mr. Johnson is the author of two books, *Dusk at the Mountain,* a study of the Negro in Washington, and *The Bay of Pigs: The Leaders' Story of Brigade 2506,* a history of the Cuban invasion.

The Pulitzer award to Mr. Johnson marks the first time a father and son have won the Pulitzer Prize for reporting. His father, Malcolm Johnson, won the prize in 1949, for a series of articles in the old New York *Sun.*

Mr. Johnson lives with his family in Alexandria, Virginia.